Running

There are three types of running events... Sprints, Middle Distance, and Long Distance.

The main Sprints are:

- 100meters/metres
- 200m
- 400m

In sprints, runners start the race in a crouched position, usually from starting blocks. It's very important to get a good start in the 100m sprint – any athlete left behind at the start won't have time to catch up!

For the 200m sprint the starting places are in a diagonal line because the lanes have different curves. The diagonal line looks strange, but it is fair to everyone.

Runners need to plan their race for the 400m sprint. They might save their strongest running for the finish, or they might try to lead all the way.

Middle Distance races are:

- 800m
- 1,500m
- 3,000m

These races start from a curved line along the track. After the start, everyone tries to get to the inside track because it has the shortest distance to the finish line.

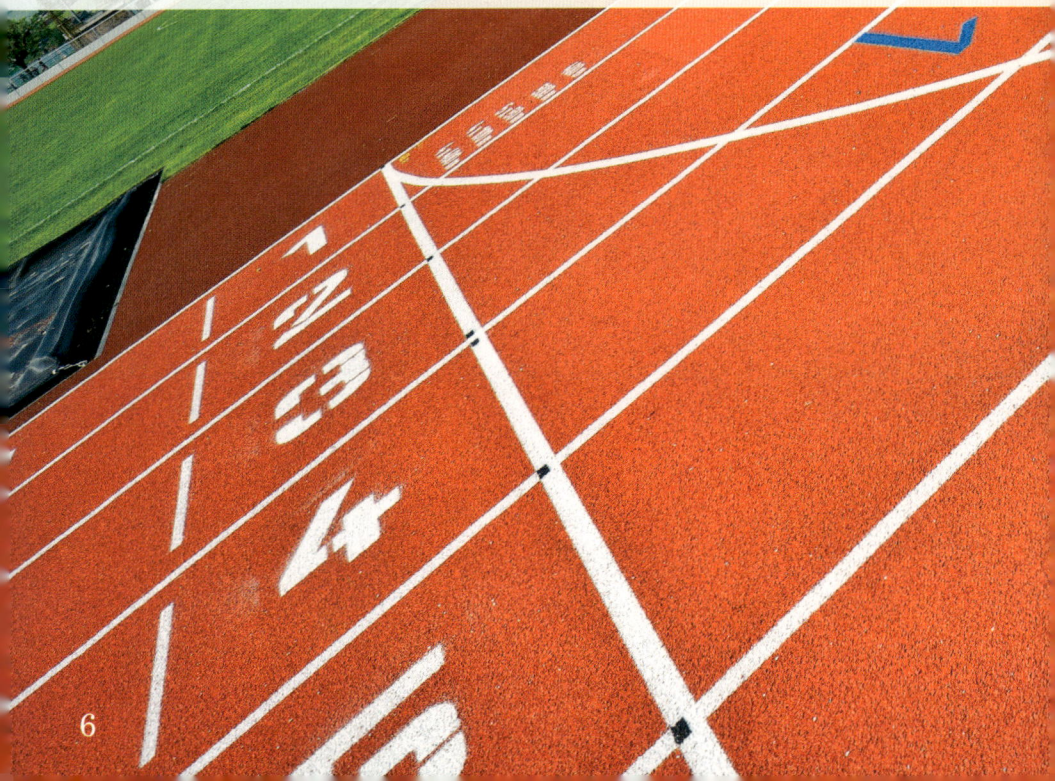

Long Distance races are:

- 5,000m
- 10,000m

Long distance running is hard work. Athletes learn how to train for these long races. To make their legs strong they may need to go to the gym, or to run up hills. In distance running, endurance is more important than top speed.

Another popular race is the distance Race Walking event. Athletes must walk fast, but always keep one foot touching the ground.

The longest race is the marathon, which is more than 26 miles /42 kilometres long! The marathon is often run as a road race, but it is a Track and Field event. At the Olympic Games everyone cheers as the runners enter the stadium to finish their long run.

Hurdles

For this event the runners race over obstacles called hurdles, which are a set distance apart. If a competitor knocks down a hurdle with their hand they are disqualified.

The big hurdles race is the 3,000m Steeplechase. This has a water jump too!

The Relay Race is the only team event in Track and Field competitions. There are four people in a team, and each runner sprints a set distance before handing a baton to the next runner. The baton must not be dropped! Cheering to support teammates can help a relay team to win!

Jumping

- Long Jump
- Triple Jump
- High Jump
- Pole Vault

Long Jumpers sprint along a track and jump from behind a mark on a board, into a sandpit. The jump is measured from where the sand is first touched.

Triple Jumpers take a hop, a step and a jump from the board into the sand.

Pole Vaulting is great to watch. Athletes run up, put the end of the pole in a metal box, and swing up with the pole, feet first, up and over the bar.

High Jumpers take a short run-up then take-off from one foot to jump up over a bar. As in the pole vault, the bar must not be knocked down. Luckily there are big cushions to land on because most jumpers go over head first, and backward.

Throwing

- Shot Put
- Discus
- Javelin
- Hammer Throw

For the Shot Put athletes "put" a heavy metal ball, called a shot, as far as they can. Throwing the shot is not allowed. Instead it is held near the neck and pushed out into the air. Strength and muscle are needed for the Shot Put, but most important is technique.

The Javelin looks easy, but the athletes have to learn to throw the light spear properly so that it travels a long way.

Technique is important for the Discus Throw, too. The heavy metal discus lies against the thrower's hand and wrist, with the fingers holding it. After about $1^{1}/_{2}$ quick turns across a circle the discus is let go, and it flies into the field.

The Hammer Throw starts from inside a cage. A steel ball joined by a wire to a steel handle is swung round and round, then let go out through the cage door. In all throwing events the longest throw wins!

- In the Middle Ages soldiers held competitions for throwing cannon balls.
- The first javelin throwers were hunters needing food.
- The ancient Greeks made discuses from lead, bronze, iron or stone.
- The marathon is so long because a Greek soldier once ran that far to deliver a message of victory.

Combined events

- Decathlon
- Heptathlon
- Pentathlon

The Decathlon has ten events: 100m, 400m, 1500m, 110m Hurdles, Long Jump, High Jump, Pole Vault, Shot Put, Discus, and Javelin. Some athletes prefer the Heptathlon, which has seven events, or the Pentathlon with five events.

In a Combined Event a score is given for each event. The highest total score wins!

Imagine all the skills athletes need to compete in a combined event!